40 Days of Biblical Declarations:

Advancing From Test to Testimony Through the Activation of God's Word

Kimberly Jones

DEDICATION

I give thanks to my Heavenly Father who enabled me, by the
inspiration of the Holy Spirit, to create this collection of
declarations based upon His infallible, unfaltering, empowering
Word.

I dedicate this book to my family- my awesome husband,
Louis, my lovely children, Kayla and Justin; and my grandson,
Kingston, all of whom have been my greatest inspiration as a wife,
mother, grandmother.....and now, author.

TABLE OF CONTENTS

ACKNOWLEDGMENTS

My sincerest gratitude is extended to the following individuals who held my arms up during this process and never let me think for one moment that I could not do this.

Louis D. Jones, Jr. - my wonderful, loving, and supportive husband who has been my biggest cheerleader and advocate for more than 15 years… I love you honey!!

Catherine Storing - my friend, my sister and accountability partner who constantly reminded me of my deadlines and walked with me through this entire process

Stephanie Kirkland - my life coach and mentor who I refer to as "The Voice" in my head that always challenges me to think outside of the box and strive for greatness

Dr. Walter Sims - a very good friend and mentor who reminded me of the necessity to *interrupt* my life in order to get this project done and step into my true identity

FOREWORD

The latest work by Pastor Kimberly Jones, *40 Days of Biblical Declarations: Advancing From Test To Testimony Through The Activation of God's Word,* is a powerful and life-changing literary masterpiece that is a must-read for every Christian. She encourages her readers to take a strategic, yet biblical, approach to overcoming adversity, testing, and trials by consistently decreeing and declaring the word of God over their lives. She believes in the transformative power of the word of God, and has personally experienced the positive impact of using God's word as a weapon against the enemy. Having overcome many obstacles in her personal life, she is a true testament to the power of remaining steadfast and unmovable in the face of adversity.

Kimberly wrote this book for those who long to transition from a place of testing into a place of testimony. I have witnessed Kimberly tirelessly decree and declare the word of God over the lives of others with passion and zeal. She is a woman of God who finds joy and fulfillment when she sees God's people come through trials and testing as victors versus victims. It is no surprise to me that she has written this book for you to add to your arsenal of weapons that will empower you to live each day victoriously.

I've heard Kimberly say on many occasions that the Bible is the best self-help and personal development book to be written since the beginning of time. This is evident as she invests in the lives of others through her various roles as a co-pastor, life coach, mentor, and spiritual counselor. No matter what hat she finds herself wearing, she emphatically employs biblical principles to counsel and coach others into victorious living. Pastor Jones possesses an unshakeable faith in the ability of God's word to renew and transform the lives of those who are striving for more.

As you go through each day of this 40-day journey, keep in mind that each of these declarations has been birthed from a place of fervent prayer and intimate meditation. As you digest the fruit created by the words of these declarations, get ready to experience supernatural strength and health in your life. It is my firm belief that after these 40 days of decreeing and declaring the word of God, you will be transformed! You will be renewed! You will be empowered! Your outlook will turn into an "uplook," and your world will be made better as a result of the activation of these biblical declarations! My hat's off to this woman of God who has opened the way for so many to transition from "test to testimony" through the power of God's word.

Dr. Walter Sims

INTRODUCTION

Creating Our World with God's Word

*A man's belly shall be satisfied with the fruit **of his** mouth; and with the **increase of his lips** shall he be filled. Death and life are in the power of the tongue; and they that love it shall eat the fruit thereof.*

Proverbs 18:20-21

The word of God is very clear regarding the power of the tongue and our ability to *create our worlds with our words.* Proverbs 18:20-21 provides a very precise description of how words can either build up or tear down one's very existence. The word of God communicates that our intangible words are capable of producing very tangible results. The level of satisfaction that we experience in our lives is directly connected to what we speak out of our mouths. We have the power to create the lives we desire by simply choosing to speak the proper words. In the natural sense, our health is seriously impacted by what we eat. If our diet is bad, then our health will suffer. The same is true in spiritual matters. If our communication is characterized by doubt and fear, we will see those things manifest in our lives. We will suffer due to the bad fruit produced by our words. On the contrary, if we speak words of faith, hope, and peace, we position ourselves for healthy physical and spiritual living. Our words serve as the key that unlocks the door to the abundant life that God desires for us.

Let's look at the Amplified version of this scripture. It reads, "A man's moral self shall be filled with the fruit of his mouth, and with the consequences of his words he must be satisfied whether good or evil." Again, the scripture is very clear about the consequences that come along with our selection of words. Whatever we put in is what we will get out. Garbage in; garbage out. Treasures in; treasures out. The condition of our lives is a reflection of fruit of the words we have eaten.

Most of us have had the unpleasant experience of eating a meal that did not sit well with our digestive system. I vividly recall this happening to me after eating a meal at one of my favorite restaurants several years ago. While I was eating the meal everything was fine, and I had no complaints. While I was eating there were no signs of any problems whatsoever. However, once I left the restaurant and returned home, it was a different story. All of a sudden my stomach began cramping and I became very nauseated. I knew immediately that my discomfort and pain came from the meal I had just eaten. The food I had eaten was bad, and I was feeling the effects of food poisoning. I can remember rolling around on the floor asking God to make it all go away and vowing to never eat at that restaurant again. After several hours of excruciating pain and torment, I finally felt some relief. The pain subsided; the food poisoning had run its course. As much as I wanted relief earlier, I had no choice but to suffer the pain until the bad food was out of my system. That's the way it is with our words. When we choose to speak words of negativity and doubt, we are taking in toxins that will eventually produce pain and suffering in our lives. Many times we wonder why we are not seeing the blessings and promises of God manifest on our behalf. It's because we have not eaten the good fruit of God's word that produces His blessings. Remember, your belly will be filled with the increase of your lips. There are great consequences when we arbitrarily speak whatever comes into our minds without any filters. Eventually, the consequences of your words will begin to show up in your life. Your spiritual, physical, relational, and emotional positioning will tell the story. If all of these areas of your life are chaotic, take a moment and reflect upon what you have spoken. If you have not been careful with your words, you may be reaping what you have sown. Just like my experience with the food poisoning, as badly as you want life's pains to go away, nothing will change until you get rid of the toxins you've ingested through negative words. Many times, we don't even realize that it is our own words that are keeping us down and preventing us from advancing into the bright future that has been ordained for us before the beginning of time. *"But thanks be unto God who always causes us to triumph in Christ Jesus!"* (II Corinthians 2:14) It is not too late to turn things around! We have the opportunity to transform our lives by making better choices in what we speak on a daily basis. Remember, changing your words will change your world!

The fact that we have this type of creative power in our tongue to change our world is founded in our spiritual identity. Think about it - when God created the world we presently live in, He did so by simply speaking. In Genesis, we see that time after time God spoke…..and it was. Hebrews 11:3 states *"Through faith we understand that the worlds were framed by the word of God, so that the things which are seen were not made of things which do appear."* Seeing that we have been created in the image and after the likeness of God, it is not unusual that we would have the same creative ability in our words. In Isaiah 57:19, the word tells us that God creates the fruit of our lips. That's powerful. Think about it. When we speak a thing, God's power comes in and actualizes it. That is too much power to handle carelessly. It's like carrying around a loaded weapon without the safety on. At any given moment, the thing that is supposed to protect and empower us could be the very thing that brings great harm to ourselves and others. There is a level of responsibility that comes along with such power. We must always remember the level of power we possess and the delegated authority we have been given on the earth. Just like that gun, if we are not careful our words can cause great damage to ourselves and others without the proper precautions in place. We must always be mindful of the fact that there is literally life and death in our tongues. It is amazing how so many individuals, who confess to be children of God, just flippantly allow words of death and destruction to leave their mouths without a second thought. We say things such as, "I am never going to get well," "I am always going to be broke," "I am never going to find the love of my life," "I can't ever do anything right," or "I'm just a failure.". All of these negative words are the fruit by which we will create either triumph or tragedy in our lives.

The book of Job asserts that we can decree a thing and it will be established unto us and the light shall shine upon our ways (Job 22:28). Again, here is a scripture that affirms our ability to create the kind of life that we desire through the creative power of our words. A decree is an official order released by legal authority. So in essence, as the people of God, we have the power to release official orders into the atmosphere based upon the legal authority that has been delegated to us by God. Psalms 8:6 tells us that man has been given authority over the works of God's hands. Essentially, we have been delegated as legal authority in the earth realm. This authority gives us the power to speak a thing and see it manifest.

By this time you may be asking yourself "What does all of this have to do with your ability to advance from test to testimony as indicated in the book's title?" This book is actually the remedy for all of those days you have spent speaking doom, gloom, and despair over your life. This book will provide you with a strategy for turning your life around by simply adopting the habit of saying about yourself what God says about you. This book is designed to equip you with the tools that will allow you to appropriately activate your authority through the proper usage of God's word. The word of God is the most powerful weapon that we have against the enemy. We can cry out to God and complain about our problems until we have no more tears to shed. It is not until we begin to decree and declare God's own words into our atmosphere that we will see the hand of God move on our behalf.

There are specifically 40 days' worth of declarations included in this book. It is very important that you understand that I did not arbitrarily pull a number out of a hat, but deliberately selected this number due to its significance. The number 40 is the number of testing, trial or probation. It is my belief that after you consistently confess these declarations over your life and the lives of your family members for the next 40 days, you will experience significant victory. I believe that as you activate your faith through decreeing and declaring the word of God, you are going to experience a supernatural turnaround in your life.

There are many instances in the Bible where there were great victories after 40 days or years of great opposition, trial or testing. Jesus went into the wilderness and was tempted by the devil for 40 days right before His ministry began. The children of Israel wandered in the wilderness for 40 years before they finally entered into their land of promise. Moses hid in the wilderness of Midian for 40 years before actually stepping into his role as the mighty deliverer who would lead the children of Israel out of a 400-year period of bondage. But what is common in all of these times of testing and trial is that after the cycle of 40 days or 40 years, there was a breakthrough. I believe that as you consistently decree and declare the word of God over yourself, your household, your family, your job, your business, or ministry for the next 40 days, you are going to experience a supernatural turnaround in your life. God is not a respecter of person. If He did great things for others after 40 days, He will surely do it for you.

Hebrews 4:12 (Amplified) *For the Word that God speaks is alive and full of power (making it active, operative, energizing, and effective); it is sharper than any two-edged sword, penetrating to the dividing line of the breath of life (soul) and (the immortal) spirit, and of the joints and marrow (of the deepest parts of our nature), exposing and sifting and analyzing and judging the very thoughts and purposes of the heart.*

Finally, as we investigate this scripture in Hebrews we can solidify the importance and power of the word of God. We must employ the strategy of decreeing the word of God based upon our belief that the word of God is not the word of man. In the book of Thessalonians, Paul commended the church because of their ability to receive the preached word, not as the word of man, but as it is in truth....The Word Of God (I Thessalonians 2:13). I love this scripture because it reveals the importance of receiving and utilizing the word of God from the perspective of that which makes it powerful, effective, energizing, and active as noted in Hebrews 4:12. The word carries all of those attributes due to the fact that it is indeed the word of God. When handled from that viewpoint, we can expect to see great results as we release His words from our mouths into the atmosphere. We begin to form those things that we see, by those things (words) that we do not see. This has nothing to do with our natural ability, but it has everything to do with the supernatural ability that coincides with God's spoken word.

This is your season to come out of your wilderness and walk into your promise! This is the season for you to walk into your position of purpose and destiny! This is the season that God wants to place you strategically into His plans and use you for His glory. He called you according to His own purpose and grace given through Jesus Christ even before the beginning of the world (II Timothy 1:9). I implore you to approach these next 40 days as if your life depended upon it, because in all actuality your life does depend upon it. Remember where we started, Proverbs 18:21 - *Life and death are in the power of the tongue, and they that love it shall eat the fruit thereof.* I believe that as you begin to "eat" the word of God each day and start releasing it over your life you are going to experience a level of liberty that will free you from whatever it is that has you bound. After these 40 days your test will become your testimony. So, get ready! You are going to be drawn closer to God as you decree and declare His undisputable word. Now brace yourself for the best 40 days ever as you transform your world through your confessions of faith according to God's word!

HOW TO USE THIS BOOK

1. Establish a set time each day for praying and confessing these declarations. Consistency is key in getting the maximum benefit from *40 Days of Biblical Declarations: Advancing from Test to Testimony Through The Activation of God's Word*. Note: A good practice to adopt is confessing your declarations when you get up in the morning and before you retire for the evening!

2. Speak each of the day's 10 declarations out loud, and ask the Holy Spirit to release revelation concerning that particular scripture. Believe that God will reveal His will for your life to you as you confess His word.

3. Ask God to show you how to practically apply the spiritual principles that are being decreed and declared into your day!

4. As you speak each declaration, do so with boldness and authority. Again, make sure that you are speaking them out loud, and not just reading them. You may even want to repeat each declaration multiple times until it resonates in your mind and your spirit.

5. Find a time during the day to actually go to each scripture in the Bible and read it in its entirety. Begin journaling each day in order to retain those things that are revealed and any instruction that you may get during your time of prayer and while you are decreeing and declaring.

6. Make sure you take your declarations with you as you go about your daily routine. Have them readily available to read and

repeat throughout your day. The more you repeat the declarations, the more of a reality they will become to you. Take a picture of them with your phone so you can easily access them. You may also want to use your phone to record yourself as you decree and declare. This way you can listen to yourself repeatedly throughout your day.

7. Declaration number 1 is the same for each day; Psalm 118:24. This is the day which the Lord has made, I shall rejoice and be glad in it!! It is imperative that you begin your declarations by rejoicing and being glad in the day that the Lord has made. No matter how you might feel as you begin your declarations, establish your positive attitude right from the start. Get excited about the possibilities of the new day and the fact that you have received a personal invitation and been given a fresh start from God Himself.

8. Declaration number 8 for each day is designated as the Declaration of Your New Beginning. The number 8 is actually the number that represents NEW BEGINNINGS! Remember, each day God gives us new mercies based on His compassion for us. Embrace the newness of each day and your ability to advance into uncharted territory in the spiritual and the natural sense. Get excited when you decree and declare your Declaration of New Beginning.

9. Declaration number 10 is the declaration that "Seals The Deal" each day. Get excited about declaration number 10, because this declaration will always give you hope and strengthen your faith in what you have just spoken over your life. This declaration affirms the fact that the word of God is true and that it will be

performed in your life!

10. Share the declarations with those individuals you come in contact with throughout the day. Tell someone else about the power of the word of God. Take every opportunity to speak the word over someone else's life!!

Enjoy!!

Pastor Kimberly Jones

Day One

1. Psalm 118:24 – This is the day which the Lord hath made, I will rejoice and be glad in it!

2. Psalms 16:11 – Today, I will stay close to God, because in His presence is fullness of joy and at His right hand are pleasures for evermore!

3. Isaiah 25:1 – Today, I choose to exalt God and praise His name for the wonderful things He has done in my life!

4. Isaiah 58:8 – I decree that light is breaking forth in my life as the morning and my health is springing forth speedily because God's glory is upon me!

5. Proverbs 3:26 – I decree that the Lord is my confidence and He will keep me from the hands of the enemy!

6. II Corinthians 4:18 – Today, I will not be moved by what I see in the natural. l will only respond according to what I know according to the spirit!

7. Philippians 4:13 – I will not be defeated today, because I can do ALL things through Christ who gives me strength!

8. II Timothy 2:20 – I decree that in my new season I will present myself unto God as a vessel of honor, sanctified and meet for the master's use and I will be prepared for every good work He has for me!

9. I Timothy 2:2 – I decree that I will live a quiet and peaceable life in all godliness and honesty!

SEALING THE DEAL DECLARATION OF THE DAY!!

10. I Thessalonians 2:13- I have received these declarations today not as the word of man, but as the word of God, therefore they will effectually work in my life...because I believe!

Day Two

1. Psalms 118:24 – This is the day which the Lord hath made, I will rejoice and be glad in it!

2. Romans 8:31 – I decree that God is for me, so anything that tries to come against me in this day will fail!

3. Psalm 37:23 – Today, my steps are being ordered by God and will lead me to places that align with purpose!

4. I Peter 5: 10 – I decree that the God of grace is making me perfect, established, strengthened and settled in all that I may endure today!

5. Romans 4:21 – Today, I am fully persuaded that what God has promised me in this day and forever He is able to also perform!

6. Proverbs 3:5 – Today, I will trust in the Lord with all my heart and lean not unto my own understanding, and acknowledge Him always, knowing that He shall direct my path today!

7. Joshua 1:8 – I decree that I will experience good success today and my way will be prosperous because I am meditating on the word of God and walking in obedience to it!

8. Ecclesiastes 3:1 – I am declaring that this is my season and I am walking in my purpose according to the timing of God and will not miss my moments of opportunity today!

9. II Timothy 1:7 – Today, I embrace the power, love, and soundness of mind that God has given me and will not allow fear to hinder me today in any capacity!

SEALING THE DEAL DECLARATION OF THE DAY!!

10. Isaiah 55:11 – All of these declarations are from the word of God, and because I have spoken them out of my mouth they shall not return unto me void, but accomplish that which God pleases and prosper in my life TODAY!

Day Three

1. Psalms 118:24 – This is the day which the Lord hath made, I will rejoice and be glad in it!

2. Matthew 7:7 – God desires to give me good gifts, so today as I ask it shall be given unto me, as I seek I shall find, as I knock it shall be opened unto me!

3. Matthew 6:33 – Today, everything will be added to me that I need as I seek the kingdom of God and his righteousness FIRST!!

4. John 13: 35 – Today, I will be recognized as a disciple of Jesus Christ as I love others!

5. Romans 8:1 – Because I walk after the Spirit and not the flesh, I will not allow condemnation to overtake me today because I am IN Christ Jesus!

6. Philippians 3:13-14 – Today, I will press toward the mark for the prize of the high calling of God in Christ and not let things from my past hinder me!

7. Matthew 5:16 – Today, I will let my light shine before men that they may see my good works and give glory to my heavenly Father!!

8. Psalm 1:3 – I will bring forth my fruit in this new season of my life, and whatsoever I do shall prosper because I am planted in the right place, at the right time, doing the right thing!

9. Jeremiah 1:19 – Today, I claim victory and even though the enemy tries to fight against me, he shall NOT prevail against me because God is with me and will deliver me!!

SEALING THE DEAL DECLARATION OF THE DAY!!

10. II Chronicles 20:17 – I will not waste my time fighting in a battle I have already won. Today, I will stand still and see the salvation of the Lord that is with me!!

Day Four

1. Psalm 118:24 – This is the day which the Lord hath made, I will rejoice and be glad in it!

2. Psalms 18:2 – I decree that the Lord is my rock, my fortress, my deliverer, my strength, my buckler, my high tower and in Him will I put my trust!!

3. Ephesians 6:10-11– I decree that I am strong in the Lord and the power of His might and I claim victory and will stand over every strategy of the enemy!

4. Psalm 67:6 – Today, I choose to praise God unconditionally, and I EXPECT the earth to yield it's increase to me and the blessings of God to overtake me!

5. Psalms 1:1-2 – I decree that I am blessed and delighting myself in God's law. I refuse to walk in the counsel of the ungodly, stand in the way of sinners, or sit in the seat of the scornful!

6. Isaiah 60:1-2 – Today, my light is come and the glory of the Lord is risen upon me and will be seen upon me, and darkness will be far from me!

7. Proverbs 16:3 – Today, I commit my works unto the Lord knowing that my thoughts shall be established by Him!

8. Habakkuk 2:3 – This is my new season and the appointed time for my vision to come forth. I decree that it shall manifest NOW and there will be no delay!

9. III John 1:11 – Today, I make a conscious decision to follow that which is good and not that which is evil because I belong to God!

SEALING THE DEAL DECLARATION OF THE DAY!!

10. II Timothy 1:12 – I believe in God and His word and I am persuaded that He is able to keep that which I have committed unto Him!

Day Five

1. Psalms 118:24 – This is the day which the Lord hath made, I will rejoice and be glad in it!

2. Philippians 2:13 – God is working in me today both to will and to do of His good pleasure!

3. II Timothy 3:16-17 – I decree that I am thoroughly furnished unto all good works because I am living according to God-inspired scriptures that are good for doctrine, reproof, correction, and instruction in righteousness!

4. Psalm 118:5 – Today, if I should find myself in a place of distress and backed into a corner I will call upon the Lord and He will set me in a large place!

5. Exodus 23:25 – I will serve God today, and in return He will bless my bread and my water, and will take sickness from the midst of me!

6. Acts 16:31 – I decree that I believe on the Lord Jesus Christ, and I take comfort in knowing that I am saved along with my entire household!

7. Romans 12:2 – No matter what happens in my day, I will not conform to this world because I have a transformed mind that is able to prove the good, acceptable, and perfect will of God!

8. Joshua 1:7 – In this new season I will be strong and very courageous as I walk into obedience to God's word. I expect to be prosperous in everything that I do and everywhere that I go!

9. II Corinthians 4:17 – I decree that whatever affliction I may endure today, it is only for a moment and is producing the fullness of God's glory in me!

SEALING THE DEAL DECLARATION OF THE DAY!!

10. Ephesians 3:20 – I decree that I will see the manifestation of all that I have spoken according to the word of God, and can expect Him to do exceedingly and abundantly above all that I could ever ask or think because of the power working in me!

Day Six

1. Psalm 118:24 – This is the day that the Lord hath made, I will rejoice and be glad in it!

2. II Peter 1:3 – I decree, according to the divine power of God, I have all things that pertain to life and godliness!

3. I John 5:14-15 – Today, I have confidence in God and believe that anything that I ask today according to His will, He will hear and answer and I will have the petitions that I desire!

4. Psalm 34:15 – I decree that The eyes of the Lord are upon me today and His ears are open unto my cry!

5. John 15:16 – I decree that God has chosen me and ordained me, therefore I will bring forth fruit and my fruit will remain!

6. Romans 12:10 – I will be kind and affectionate to others today, always showing brotherly love!

7. I Corinthians 2:5 – I decree that my faith is grounded in the power of God and not the wisdom of man!

8. Isaiah 43:19 – Today, I am beholding the new thing that God is doing in my life. It will spring forth and I will know it!!

9. Hebrews 11:1 – I have NOW faith today, which is the substance of the things I am believing God for and proof of the things I have not seen, YET!

SEALING THE DEAL DECLARATION OF THE DAY!!

10. James 1:23-25 – As I look into and confess God's word, I will continue in it, never forgetting what I have heard and always doing the work it requires. Doing so will cause me to be blessed in all that I do TODAY!

Day Seven

1. Psalm 118:24 – This is the day which the Lord hath made, we will rejoice and be glad in it!

2. Psalm 138:2 – Because you have magnified your word above your name I will worship you and praise you knowing that your word is truth!

3. Psalms 19:12-13 – It is my desire that God will cleanse me from secret faults and presumptuous sins today and they will NOT have dominion over me!

4. Isaiah 30:15 – As I return and rest in the Lord I shall be saved and find strength in quietness and confidence!

5. Matthew 6:14 – Today, I walk in forgiveness towards others, knowing that God has forgiven me!

6. Hebrews 12:1 – Today, I deliberately lay aside every weight and sin which serves as a distraction to easily beset me and I run with patience the race that is set before me!

7. I Peter 1: 5-8 – Today, I operate in virtue, knowledge, temperance, patience, godliness, brotherly kindness, and charity. Therefore, I will not be barren or unfruitful in the knowledge of Jesus!

8. Ephesians 4:22&24 – Today, I put off the old man, and I put on the new man which is created in righteousness and true holiness!

9. I Samuel 15:22 – Today, I choose to be obedient to God's instructions, understanding that obedience is better than sacrifice!

SEALING THE DEAL DECLARATION OF THE DAY!!

10. Isaiah 66:9 – As I have spoken the word today, I decree that I will bring forth that which God desires to birth through me. The womb of my spirit is open and I will see manifestations in the outer world based on what is on the inside of me TODAY!!

Day Eight

1. Psalm 118:24 – This is the day which the Lord hath made, I will rejoice and be glad in it!

2. Psalm 149:6 – Today, I choose to let the high praises of God be my defense against any weapon that may be formed against me today!

3. I Chronicles 12:32 – I decree that the same spirit of discernment that was upon the children of Issachar is upon me and I will understand my seasons and make wise decisions today!

4. Nehemiah 8:10 – Today is a holy day without sorrow because I will allow the joy of the Lord to be my strength!

5. Psalm 118:5 – Today I will call upon the name of the Lord when I am in distress and He will answer me and set me in a large place!

6. Romans 8:11 – Today, I decree that I will not stay in dead places because the same spirit that raised Jesus from the dead dwells in me!

7. Philippians 2:5 – I decree that the same mind that was in Christ Jesus is also in me!

8. Ezekiel 36:26 – God is healing any hardness that may be in my heart and is giving me a new heart and a new spirit for this new season!

9. Jeremiah 29:11 – Today, God is thinking peaceful thoughts about me that will lead me into my expected end!

SEALING THE DEAL DECLARATION OF THE DAY!!

10. James 1:25 – Because I am a doer of the word of God and not a forgetful hearer, I WILL continue in these declarations that I have spoken today. I SHALL be blessed in all that I do!

Day Nine

1. Psalm 118:24 – This is the day which the Lord hath made, I will rejoice and be glad in it!

2. Colossians 1:23 – Today, my faith will remain grounded and settled and I will not be moved away from the hope of the Gospel!

3. Ephesians 6:13 – Today, as I put on the whole armour of God I am confident that I will be protected from any evil that may arise.

4. Colossians 3:1-2 – I decree that I am risen with Christ and I seek those things which are above and not the things on the earth!

5. Isaiah 43:2 – I decree that God is with me today, and I will not be flooded by rivers of problems, and I will not be burned in times of adversity!

6. Isaiah 43:1 – Today, I know who I am because God has called me by my name and created me for His glory!

7. Matthew 6:10 – I decree that that the kingdom of heaven is invading the earth and the will of God is manifesting in my life!

8. Philippians 3:13-14 – Today, as I press for the mark of the high calling that is before me, I forget those things that are behind me, and reach for those things which are ahead of me!

9. I Thessalonians 5:18 – Today, I choose to give thanks to God in everything, knowing that this is the will of God in Christ Jesus concerning me!

SEALING THE DEAL DECLARATION OF THE DAY!!

10. Hebrews 10:23 – Today, I will hold fast to the profession of my faith that I have exercised through these declarations without wavering. I can do this because I know that He is faithful that promised!

Day Ten

1. Psalm 118:24 – This is the day which the Lord hath made, I will rejoice and be glad in it!

2. Jeremiah 33:3 – As I call unto the Lord today, He will answer me and show me great and mighty things which I know not!

3. Ecclesiastes 3:11-12 – God makes everything beautiful in His time, I decree that it's my time and I will rejoice and do GOOD in my life!

4. Job 42:10 – Today, I will pray for my friends, and in doing so God will restore good things unto me!

5. Psalm 1:1 – I am blessed today because I will not walk in the counsel of the ungodly, stand in the way of sinners, nor sit in the seat of the scornful!

6. Joel 2:25 – I am in a season of restoration and I believe that the years that have been destroyed by enemies are being redeemed NOW!

7. Ecclesiastes 5:2 – Today, I will monitor what I say and I will not be rash with my mouth or hasty with my words!

8. Ezekiel 36:36 – The Lord is rebuilding ruined places in my life and allowing growth in unfruitful areas of my life. He has spoken it and will do it in this new season of my life!

9. Philippians 4:6-7 – Today, I will not fret or be anxious about anything, but in every circumstance I will make my requests known unto God with thanksgiving and be in peace!

SEALING THE DEAL DECLARATION OF THE DAY!!

10. Hebrews 11:6 – I know that without faith it is impossible to please God, therefore by FAITH I believe the word of the Lord that I have declared today will come to pass because God is a rewarder of them that diligently seek HIM!

Day Eleven

1. Psalm 118:24 – This is the day which the Lord hath made, I will rejoice and be glad in it!

2. Psalms 24:9 – Today, I will keep my head lifted up and allow the King of Glory to infiltrate every area of my life!

3. Ecclesiastes 1:13 – Today, I will seek and search out wisdom with my heart and I believe that God will reveal His will to me!

4. Isaiah 40:29 – I decree that the power and the strength of God will sustain me today when I want to faint and when I have no might!

5. Philippians 4:6-7 – Today, I will not be anxious for anything, but I will let my requests be known unto God and His peace shall be released unto me!

6. Colossians 1:13 – I decree that I have been delivered from the power of darkness and translated into the kingdom of God!

7. James 2:5 – I decree that I love God and I am an heir to His kingdom, so today I embrace my inheritance!

8. Romans 4:18-19 – In this new season I will hope against hope and will be strong in my faith, knowing that every promise God has made to me will come to pass…..No Matter What!

9. Psalm 147:14 – I decree that peace shall dwell within my borders today and God will grant His very best to me!

SEALING THE DEAL DECLARATION OF THE DAY!!

10. I Kings 8:56- I decree that every promise that God has made to me through His word will always flourish in my life and will never fail!

Day Twelve

1. Psalm 118:24 – This is the day which the Lord hath made, I will rejoice and be glad in it!

2. Psalm 119:133 – I decree that my steps are ordered in the word of the Lord today and sin will not have rule over me!

3. Isaiah 11:2 – I declare that the Spirit of the Lord will rest upon me today and I will operate in wisdom, understanding, counsel, might, knowledge, and the fear of the Lord!

4. Jeremiah 1:5 – I will walk in confidence today, knowing that God knew me, sanctified me, and ordained me for my purpose before I was even born!

5. Lamentations 3:22-23 – Life's challenges will not consume me because I am covered by the new mercies that God has given me for this day!

6. I Corinthians 15:33 – I will be aware of who I surround myself with today, knowing that evil companionship can corrupt my character and good manners!

7. Romans 12:2 – Today, I present my body as a living sacrifice, holy and acceptable unto God which is my reasonable service!

8. Jeremiah 18:4 – Today, I submit myself into the hands of God as a lump of clay asking that He make me into what He desires me to be for this new season of my life. I am ready for my makeover today!

9. Galatians 6:7 – I will sow good seeds today through my words, behaviors, and attitudes, understanding that whatever I sow that shall I reap!

SEALING THE DEAL DECLARATION OF THE DAY!!

10. **Matthew 18:18 – As I have declared the word of God today He has released keys to the kingdom to me and whatsoever I have bound and loosed with my words will be bound and loosed in the heavens! I claim my victory NOW!**

Day Thirteen

1. Psalm 118:24 – This is the day which the Lord hath made, I will rejoice and be glad in it!

2. Psalm 9:10 – I decree that I know the name of the Lord and will put my trust in Him today, believing that He will not forsake me as I seek Him!

3. Proverbs 3:1-2 – Today, I will keep God's commandments with my heart and not forget his law; in doing so I will enjoy length of days, long life, and peace!

4. Isaiah 45:3 – I decree that treasures of darkness and hidden riches of secret places are being released unto me by my God who called me by my name!

5. I Corinthians 10:13 – I will be able to withstand any temptation that presents itself to me today, knowing that God will make a way to escape!

6. Psalm 91:9-10 – No evil will come upon me or my dwelling place today because I choose to make my Lord, the most High, my refuge and habitation!

7. Isaiah 45:2 – I decree that God is going before me today and making crooked places straight and breaking through every difficult situation in my life!

8. I Corinthians 13:11 – I am walking in my new season and there is no room for childish things. My thinking and understanding are maturing as l release those immature things that do not correspond with where God is taking me!

9. Exodus 14:13 – Today I will fear not, stand still and see the salvation of the Lord which He will show me today. The enemies that I see and fight against today will no longer be an issue for me!

SEALING THE DEAL DECLARATION OF THE DAY!!

10. I John 5:14-15 – I have confidence that God has heard me as I have declared His word and His will. And because He has heard me I believe that what I have asked and desired of Him will be granted to me! TODAY!!

Day Fourteen

1. Psalm 118:24 – This is the day which the Lord hath made, I will rejoice and be glad in it!

2. James 1:19 – Today I will be swift to hear, slow to speak, and slow to wrath!

3. Luke 10:19 – Today I will triumph over all the power of the enemy because God has given me power to do so and nothing shall hurt me!

4. John 10:10 – Today I embrace the abundant life Jesus came to give me and decree that the enemy will not kill, steal, or destroy what is rightfully mine!

5. II Corinthians 9:8 – God is making all grace abound toward me that I will always have all sufficiency in all things!

6. Jeremiah 1:19 – I decree that even though the enemy may fight against me, he shall not prevail against me because God is with me! I'm victorious!!

7. John 10:27 – Today, I will recognize the voice of God and follow Him when He speaks because I am one of His sheep!

8. Isaiah 54:2-3 – God is enlarging my territory in my new season and I am making room for what He has for me, as I break forth on the right and the left!

9. Proverbs 4:7 – Today, I will get wisdom because it is the principal thing, but with all my getting I will also get understanding!

SEALING THE DEAL DECLARATION OF THE DAY!!

10. Luke 11:9 – Based upon the declarations I have made today, I expect that what I ask for will be given to me; what I seek I will find, and when I knock on God-ordained doors they shall be opened unto me!

Day Fifteen

1. Psalm 118:24 – This is the day which the Lord hath made, I will rejoice and be glad in it!

2. Psalm 56:4 – Today, I will trust God and praise His word, not fearing what man can do to me!

3. Proverbs 8:21 – Today, God will cause me to inherit substance and He will fill my treasures because I love Him!

4. Romans 8:1 – I will not live in condemnation today because I am in Christ Jesus and I walk after the Spirit and not after the flesh!

5. I Corinthians 15:10 – I decree that I am what I am by the grace of God and the grace that is on my life will not be wasted!

6. Psalm 37:4 – Today, I will delight myself in the Lord and He will give me the desires of my heart!

7. Acts 1:8 –The power of the Holy Spirit rests upon me and is empowering me to be a good witness of my Heavenly Father everywhere that I go and in all that I do!

8. II Sam 22:33- I decree that God is my strength and my power and He is making my way perfect!

9. II Corinthians 10:3-4- Today I will not war after the flesh or use carnal weapons to fight the enemy. I am pulling down and overthrowing strongholds NOW!

SEALING THE DEAL DECLARATION OF THE DAY!!

10. Isaiah 55:11 – The words that have gone out of my mouth through these declarations shall not return void, but will accomplish that which God pleases and prosper in the thing whereto it has been sent.

Day Sixteen

1. Psalm 118:24 – This is the day which the Lord hath made, I will rejoice and be glad in it!

2. I Peter 5:7 – Today, I will cast my cares upon the Lord because I know He cares for me!

3. Psalm 84:11 – I decree that no good thing will be kept from me today. As I will walk uprightly before the Lord, He will release His grace and His glory!

4. James 5:16 – Today, my prayers will be effective and fervent and will produce great power for healing in my life and in others' lives!

5. Matthew 4:4 – Today, my life will be better because I will live by every word that proceeds out of the mouth of God!

6. I Corinthians 15:58 – Today, I will be steadfast, unmovable, always abounding in the work of the Lord, believing that my work is not in vain!

7. II Corinthians 3:17 – Today, I embrace the liberty that comes along with the presence and power of the Holy Spirit that is with me!

8. Galatians 6:9 – This is my new season and this is due season and I am expecting my harvest to come forth. Therefore, I will not get weary in well doing and I will not faint!

9. I Peter 5:6 – I will humble myself under the mighty hand of God today knowing that HE will exalt me in due time!

SEALING THE DEAL DECLARATION OF THE DAY!!

10. Matthew 13:8 – I decree that I am good ground and as I have made these declarations today the word of God has taken root in me and will produce a 100, 60, and 30-fold return in my life!

Day Seventeen

1. Psalm 118:24 – This is the day which the Lord hath made, I will rejoice and be glad in it!

2. James 4:7 – Today, I will submit myself to God, resist the devil, and he will flee from me!!

3. Psalms 34:15 – I decree that I am righteous and the eyes of the Lord are upon me today and His ears are open to my cry!

4. Genesis 1:26 – I decree that I am made in the image and after the likeness of God and will exercise the dominion authority He has given me over the works of His hand!

5. Deuteronomy 8:18 – I am walking in abundance today, because God has given me the power to get wealth!

6. Proverbs 15:1 – Today, I will not allow my words to be used to stir up anger in myself or others and I will use a soft answer to turn away wrath!

7. Acts 16:25 – I am expecting a "SUDDENLY" in my life that will shake the foundation of those things that have me bound. I decree that doors of opportunity are opening for me and the enemy's bands are loosed from my life!

8. Luke 9:62 – I will keep my focus in this new season and I will not allow anything to distract me or cause me to look back and be unworthy of the kingdom of God!

9. II Corinthians 10:5 – Today, I will cast down imaginations and every high thing that exalts itself against the knowledge of God, and I will bring every thought captive to the obedience of Christ!

SEALING THE DEAL DECLARATION OF THE DAY!!

10. Romans 4:21 – I have made all of these declarations by faith and am fully persuaded that God is able to perform everything He has promised me!

Day Eighteen

1. Psalm 118:24 – This is the day which the Lord hath made, I will rejoice and be glad in it!

2. Psalm 19:14 – I decree that the words of my mouth and the meditations of my heart are acceptable in the sight of the Lord who is my strength and my redeemer!

3. II Chronicles 16:9 – I decree that the Lord will show Himself strong on my behalf today because my heart is perfect toward Him!

4. Isaiah 38:17 – Because the Lord loves me, He will deliver my soul from corruption and cast all my sins behind His back!

5. Matthew 7:11 – I decree that my heavenly Father is releasing good gifts to me today, as I ask by faith!

6. Romans 4:20 – Today, I will not stagger at the promises of God through unbelief, but I have strong faith and will always give God the glory!

7. Ephesians 2:6 – I decree that I am seated in heavenly places with Christ Jesus who has raised me up!

8. Proverbs 18:16 - In my new season, my gift is making room for me and bringing me before great men!

9. Titus 1:16 – I will profess that I know God today and I will not deny Him in my works!

SEALING THE DEAL DECLARATION OF THE DAY!!

10. Numbers 23:19 – All of the declarations I have made today will come to pass because God is not a man that He should lie nor son of man that He should repent. He said it and He will do it. He has spoken it and will make it good!

Day Nineteen

1. Psalm 118:24 – This is the day which the Lord hath made, I will rejoice and be glad in it!

2. James 4:8 – I decree that as I draw near to God today, He will draw near to me!

3. 3 John 1:2 – Today, I will prosper in my mind, my will and my emotions and I am in good health!

4. Romans 8:38-39 – I decree that today absolutely NOTHING will separate me from the love of God, which is in Christ Jesus!

5. Psalm 27:1 – I decree that the Lord is my light, my salvation, and the strength of my life; therefore, I will not fear nor be afraid of anything this day might bring my way!

6. Matthew 17: 20 – I have big faith and will exercise it by speaking to any mountain that is presented in this day and it will move at my command! Nothing will be impossible for me TODAY!

7. II Chronicles 20:27 – I will have joy today because the Lord will make me rejoice over my enemies!

8. I Kings 19:11-12 – In my new season I will not be distracted and will carefully listen for the still small voice of God as He gives me insight and direction into the new place He has ordained for me!

9. Proverbs 18:10 – I decree that the name of the Lord is my strong tower and I will run into it and find safety!

SEALING THE DEAL DECLARATION OF THE DAY!!

10. Psalm 119:105 – I decree that the word of God is a lamp unto my feet and a light unto my path. These declarations I have made today will illuminate all the dark places in my life and provide guidance and direction for me in all I do today!

Day Twenty

1. Psalm 118:24 – This is the day which the Lord hath made, I will rejoice and be glad in it!

2. Philippians 4:8 – Today, I will be mindful of my thoughts and will only think on those things that are true, honest, just, pure, lovely, and of a good report according to the will of God!

3. Isaiah 1:19 – Today, I will be willing and obedient to God and I will eat the good of the land!

4. Jeremiah 1:7 – Today, I will be yielded to God and go as He sends and speak what He commands!

5. Ezekiel 36:26-27 – Today, my spirit is being renewed and my heart is receptive to walking in and keeping God's instruction!

6. Proverbs 8:21 – I decree that I love the Lord, and He is filling my treasure and causing me to inherit substance!

7. Romans 12:21 – Today, I will not be overcome with evil, but I will overcome evil with good!

8. Philippians 4:13 – I decree that in this new season I will not back down or run from challenges. I understand my ability to do all things through Christ who strengthens me in this season!

9. Proverbs 8:17 – I decree that the Lord loves me and I love Him and I will always find Him as I seek Him early!

SEALING THE DEAL DECLARATION OF THE DAY!!

10. Jeremiah 29:12-13 – I decree that as I call on the Lord today and pray according to these declarations that He will hear me. I will continue to seek the Lord today with my whole heart, and I will find Him!

Day Twenty One

1. Psalm 118:24 – This is the day which the Lord hath made, I will rejoice and be glad in it!

2. Romans 8:37 – Today, I claim victory in all that I do because I am more than a conqueror through Him that loves me!

3. John 16:33 – Today, I will have peace and I will be of good cheer in the midst of trouble because Jesus has already overcome every challenge I will face!

4. Isaiah 55:8 – I will follow God even when I don't understand His plan, knowing that my thoughts are not His thoughts and my ways are not His ways!

5. Psalms 34:1 – Today, I will bless the Lord at all times and His praise shall continually be in my mouth!

6. II Corinthians 12:9 – I decree that God's grace is sufficient for me and His strength is made perfect in my weakness!

7. I John 4:4 – I decree that I will not be defeated today because greater is He that is in me than he that is in the world!

8. John 15:16 – I decree that I have been chosen and ordained to bring forth fruit in this season that will remain. And whatever I ask of the Father, according to His will in Jesus name, will be given unto me!

9. Hebrews 10:36 – I decree that I will have patience as I operate in God's will today, knowing that I will receive His promises!

SEALING THE DEAL DECLARATION OF THE DAY!!

10. II Corinthians 1:20 – I am assured that these declarations that I have made today, according to the word of God, will surely come to pass because all of the promises of God are in Him YES and AMEN!

Day Twenty Two

1. Psalm 118:24 – This is the day which the Lord hath made, I will rejoice and be glad in it!

2. II Chronicles 19:9 – I decree that everything that I do today I will do in the fear of the Lord, faithfully, and with a perfect heart!

3. Psalm 84:11 – I decree that no good thing will be withheld from me today, as I walk upright before the Lord!

4. John 14:27 – The peace that I have comes from God and not the world, therefore I will not allow my heart to be troubled today and I will not be afraid!

5. Psalms 51:6 – I decree that today I will operate in truth and wisdom from the innermost part of my being!

6. Isaiah 43:7 – I decree that God has called me, formed me, made me and created me for His glory!

7. Psalms 149:6 – I decree that today the high praises of God will be in my mouth and a two-edged sword in my hand, as I triumph over the enemy!

8. Romans 8:28 – In this season I decree that all things are working together for my good because I love God and have been called according to His purpose!

9. John 13:35 – Today, I will be recognized as a disciple of Christ based upon the love that I show to others!

SEALING THE DEAL DECLARATION OF THE DAY!!

10. Luke 1:45 – I decree that I am blessed and I believe that there shall be a performance of the things that God has spoken through these declarations I have made today!

Day Twenty Three

1. Psalm 118:24 – This is the day which the Lord hath made, I will rejoice and be glad in it!

2. James 4:7 – Today, as I submit myself to God, stand firm and resist the devil, he must flee from me!

3. Psalm 91:1 – Today, I will dwell in the secret place of the Most High and remain stable and fixed under the shadow of the Almighty!

4. Hebrew 13:6 – I decree that the Lord is my helper and I will not fear what man can do to me!

5. Luke 9:23 – Today, as I pursue Jesus, I will deny myself, take up my cross, and follow Him!

6. Matthew 11:12 – I decree that I have the strength to take by force everything that God has promised me!

7. Deuteronomy 6:5 – Today, I will love the Lord my God with all my heart, soul, and might!

8. Joel 2:28 – In this new season I will be used mightily of God as He releases a fresh outpouring of His spirit upon my life!

9. Philippians 1:6 – I am confident that God will perform the work in me that He has begun until the day of Jesus Christ!

SEALING THE DEAL DECLARATION OF THE DAY!!

10. I John 3:22- I decree that whatsoever I have asked of the Lord today I will receive from him because I am obedient unto his commandments and do those things that are pleasing in His sight.

Day Twenty Four

1. Psalm 118:24 – This is the day which the Lord hath made, I will rejoice and be glad in it!

2. James 4:10 – Today, I will humble myself in the sight of the Lord, knowing that He will lift me up!

3. Matthew 16:18-19 – Today, the gates of hell will not prevail against me as I use the keys of the kingdom to bind on earth what is bound in heaven and loose on earth what has been loosed in heaven!

4. Psalm 41:11 – I decree that God's favor is on my life and the enemy will not triumph over me!

5. Isaiah 57:19 – Because God creates the fruit of my lips, I will only speak blessings over my life and say about myself what God says about me!

6. I Peter 2:9 – Today, I will show forth my praise unto God who has called me out of darkness into his marvelous light!

7. Psalm 1:2 – I decree that I will delight in the law of the Lord today and meditate upon His word both day and night!

8. Ephesians 3:20 – I decree that in this season I will experience increase because my God will do exceedingly and abundantly more in my life than I could ever ask or think because I have His power working in me!

9. Psalm 34:10 – I decree that I will not lack or want any good thing today because I will seek the Lord!

SEALING THE DEAL DECLARATION OF THE DAY!!

10. I Peter 1:25 – I decree that the words that I have declared today are God's words, and they will continually work and manifest good things in my life because the word of the Lord endures forever!

Day Twenty Five

1. Psalm 118:24 – This is the day which the Lord hath made, I will rejoice and be glad in it!

2. Deuteronomy 28:2 – I decree that the blessings of the Lord will come on me and overtake me today as I hearken unto the voice of my God!

3. Acts 16:31 – I decree that as I believe on the Lord Jesus Christ I will be saved along with my entire household!

4. John 1:12 – Because I have received Him and believe on the name of Lord Jesus Christ, He has given me the power to become a son/daughter of His!

5. II Corinthians 2:14 – I decree that today God will cause me to triumph in Christ and I will make His presence known everywhere I go!

6. Psalm 103:2-5 – Today, I will bless the Lord and will not forget any of His benefits! (He forgives my sins, heals all of my diseases, saves me from destruction, crowns me with loving kindness and tender mercies, satisfies my mouth with good things and renews my youth like the eagle's!)

7. Psalms 118:6 – I decree that the Lord is on my side and I will not fear what man can do to me!

8. Romans 8:18 – I decree that the sufferings of this present time are not worthy to be compared with the glory which shall be revealed in me in my new season!

9. II Corinthians 12:9 – I decree that the power of Christ is resting upon me no matter what I face because His strength is made perfect in my weakness!

SEALING THE DEAL DECLARATION OF THE DAY!!

10. John 17:17 – I decree that the words I have spoken today are truth because they are the words of God and they will sanctify, purify, consecrate, separate me unto God, and make me holy!!

Day Twenty Six

1. Psalm 118:24 – This is the day which the Lord hath made, I will rejoice and be glad in it!

2. Romans 8:11 – I decree that the Spirit of Him that raised Jesus from the dead dwells in me and will restore me to life today!

3. Nehemiah 8:10 – Today is a holy day unto the Lord and I will not be down, depressed or discouraged because the joy of the Lord is my strength!

4. Ephesians 4:29 – I will not allow any corrupt communication to come out of my mouth today and will speak only that which is good in order to edify and minister to those that hear me!

5. Ephesians 6:13 – Today, I will STAND and put on the whole armour of God that I may be able to withstand any evil that this day may present!

6. Psalm 126:2 – Today, my mouth will be filled with laughter and my tongue shall be filled with singing because the Lord shall do great things for me!

7. Proverbs 24:3 – I decree that I will use wisdom and understanding to establish my life, home, and family!

8. Isaiah 43:18-19 – I will forget the former things and the things of old because God is doing a new thing in my life in this season. He will make a way in the wilderness and create rivers in the desert!

9. Joshua 24:15 – I decree that I and my entire household will serve the Lord!

SEALING THE DEAL DECLARATION OF THE DAY!!

10. Matthew 13:23 – Today, I have received the seed of the word upon the good ground of my heart. I have heard it, understood it and expect it to bring forth abundant fruit of a hundred, sixty, and thirty-fold return!

Day Twenty Seven

1. Psalm 118:24 – This is the day which the Lord hath made, I will rejoice and be glad in it!

2. Isaiah 12:2 – I decree that God is my salvation, my strength and my song; I will trust Him and not be afraid!

3. III John 1:11 – Today I will follow after those things which are good and not evil because I belong to God!

4. Philippians 3:3 – Today, I will worship God in spirit, rejoice in Jesus Christ, and have no confidence in my flesh!

5. Hebrews 11:6 – I decree that by faith I believe that God is who He says He is and that He will reward me as I diligently seek Him; for without faith it is impossible to please Him!

6. Psalms 31:15 – I decree that my times are in the hands of the Lord and He will deliver me from the hand of my enemies and those that persecute me!

7. II Peter 1:8 – I decree that I will never be barren nor unfruitful in the knowledge of my Lord Jesus Christ!

8. I Corinthians 16:9 – I decree that a wide door of opportunity is opening for me in this season and I will be aware of all opposition!

9. Isaiah 61:7 – I decree that God is giving me double for any shame and confusion I have endured in the past and I shall have everlasting joy!

SEALING THE DEAL DECLARATION OF THE DAY!!

10. Numbers 23:19 – Because I know that God is not a man that He should lie, neither son of man that He should repent, I am confident that what He has said He will do and what He has spoken through these declarations He will make good!

Day Twenty Eight

1. Psalm 118:24 – This is the day which the Lord hath made, I will rejoice and be glad in it!

2. Isaiah 11:2 – I decree that the Spirit of the Lord rests upon me and will produce wisdom and knowledge, counsel and strength, knowledge and the fear of the Lord in my life!

3. Proverbs 1:33 – Today, I will dwell in safety and shall be quiet from fear of evil as I hearken unto the wisdom of God!

4. Micah 7:19 – I decree that God will have compassion upon me, subdue my iniquities and cast my sins into the depths of the sea!

5. Matthew 5:14 – I decree that I am a light in the world and as a city on a hill that cannot be hid.

6. Romans 12:12 – Today, I will rejoice in hope, have patience in tribulation, and remain consistent in prayer!

7. Isaiah 45:3 – I decree that God is giving me the treasures of darkness and hidden riches of secret places so that I may know that He is God!

8. Habakkuk 2:3 – I decree that this is my appointed time and my vision will speak in this season and not lie. I will wait because it shall surely come to pass!

9. Luke 1:28 – I decree that I am highly favored and blessed because the Lord is with me!

SEALING THE DEAL DECLARATION OF THE DAY!!

10. II Timothy 3:16 – I decree that the scriptures that I have declared today are given by the inspiration of God. They are profitable in my life for doctrine, reproof, correction, and instruction in righteousness, making me perfect and thoroughly furnished unto all good works!

Day Twenty Nine

1. Psalm 118:24 – This is the day which the Lord hath made, I will rejoice and be glad in it!

2. John 12:46 – Jesus is my light today and because I believe in Him I will never dwell in darkness!

3. II Timothy 4:18 – The Lord shall deliver me from every evil work and will preserve me unto His heavenly kingdom!

4. Colossians 3:23 – I decree that whatever I do today I will do heartily as unto the Lord and not men!

5. I Corinthians 15:10 – I decree that it is by the grace of God that I am what I am and His grace was not bestowed upon me in vain!

6. Deuteronomy 30:16 – Today, I will love the Lord, walk in His ways, and keep His commandments, believing that I will live and multiply and be blessed in my place of promise!

7. II Chronicles 20:20 – Today, I will be established as I believe in the Lord and I will prosper as I believe in His prophets!

8. Isaiah 6:8 – I decree that in this new season as I hear the voice of the Lord calling, my response will be "Here am I. Send me!"

9. Psalm 138:7 – Today, should I walk in the midst of trouble, I decree that the Lord will revive me and save me as He protects me from mine enemies!

SEALING THE DEAL DECLARATION OF THE DAY!!

10. Matthew 24:34-35 – I decree that the declarations I have made today shall be fulfilled because the word of God shall never pass away!

Day Thirty

1. Psalm 118:24 – This is the day which the Lord hath made, I will rejoice and be glad in it!

2. Isaiah 26:3 - I decree perfect peace over my life today as I keep my mind stayed upon the Lord!

3. Romans 5:8 - Today, I embrace the love of God that was shown toward me through the sacrifice of Jesus Christ while I was yet a sinner!

4. Revelation 12:11 - Today, I will overcome the enemy by the word of my testimony and by the blood of the lamb!

5. Matthew 26:41 - Today, I will watch and pray and be very aware of temptations that may try and overtake me!

6. Psalms 8:6 - I decree that I have dominion authority over the works of God's hands and all things are under my feet!

7. Proverbs 18:21 - I decree that the power of life and death is in my tongue. Therefore, I will choose my words wisely today!

8. Ezekiel 36:26 - I decree that in my new season God is giving me a new heart and a new spirit that I may always be in right standing with Him as I walk in my purpose and destiny!

9. II Timothy 1:9 - I decree that I have been saved and called by God according to His own purpose and grace which was given to me in Jesus Christ before the world began!

SEALING THE DEAL DECLARATION OF THE DAY!!

10. Romans 4:20-21 - I am fully persuaded that He is able to perform all that He has promised through these declarations and I will not stagger at His promises!

Day Thirty One

1. Psalm 118:24 – This is the day which the Lord hath made, I will rejoice and be glad in it!

2. Psalm 118:17 – I decree that I shall not die, but live and declare the works of the Lord!

3. Romans 8:31 – I speak to every difficult situation in my life and declare that God is FOR me so who can be against me!4. Psalm 51:10 – I decree that God is creating in me a clean heart and renewing a right spirit within me right NOW!

5. II Corinthians 3:17 – Today, I will walk in liberty because the Spirit of the Lord is with me and in me!

6. John 5:30 – Today, I will not seek my own will but the will of the Father who is sending me forth, realizing I can do nothing without Him!

7. Psalm 37:25 – I decree that I am the righteousness of God and I will not be forsaken and my seed will never beg for bread!

8. Proverbs 8:12 – I decree that in this new season of my life the wisdom and creativity of God has been released and activated in me and will reveal unto me witty inventions through divine inspiration!

9. Philippians 4:19 – I decree that my God shall supply all my needs according to His riches in glory by Christ Jesus!

SEALING THE DEAL DECLARATION OF THE DAY!!

10. Hebrews 6:12 – I will possess and inherit the promises of these declarations through faith and patience as I continue to follow God!

Day Thirty Two

1. Psalm 118:24 – This is the day which the Lord hath made, I will rejoice and be glad in it!

2. I Timothy 6:11 – Today, I will follow after righteousness, godliness, faith, love, patience and meekness!

3. II Thessalonians 3:1 – I decree that the word of God will have free course in my life today!

4. I Timothy 2:2 – Today, I will lead a quiet and peaceable life in godliness and honesty!

5. Colossians 1:23 – Today, I will be grounded and settled in my faith and will not be moved away from the hope of the Gospel!

6. 2 Corinthians 9:8 – I decree that God is able to make all grace abound toward me and I will always have all sufficiency in all things!

7. Psalms 9:10 – I will seek the Lord today and trust Him, knowing that He will not forsake me!

8. Ecclesiastes 3:1 – I know that there is a season and a time to every purpose under heaven and I decree that this is the season and the time for my life to change and for my purpose to come forth!

9. II Corinthians 10:5 – Today, I will cast down imagination and every high thing that exalts itself against the knowledge of God and bring every thought captive to the obedience of Christ!

SEALING THE DEAL DECLARATION OF THE DAY!!

10. I John 5:14-15 – I have confidence in God and I know that He has heard me today because I have asked according to His will and He will give me that which I desire of Him!

Day Thirty Three

1. Psalm 118:24 – This is the day which the Lord hath made, I will rejoice and be glad in it!

2. Jeremiah 29:11 – I decree that God is thinking thoughts of peace and not of evil about me and has given me an expected end!

3. John 14:21 – I decree that God will manifest Himself unto me today because I love Him and I am obedient to His commands!

4. I John 5:4 – Today, I confess that I am born of God and through my faith I will overcome anything this world may present today!

5. I Peter 2:9 – I decree that I am chosen of God and I will show forth the praises of Him who called me out of darkness into His marvelous light!

6. II Corinthians 4:17 – I decree that this light affliction I am dealing with today is but for a moment and is working out something far greater in me!

7. I John 4:4 – Today, I will be victorious in all that I do because greater is He that is in me than He that is in the world!

8. I Corinthians 2:9 – I decree that I love God, and eye hath not seen nor ear heard neither have it entered into the heart of man the things that He has prepared for me in this new season!

9. Psalm 119:105 – Today, the word of the Lord will serve as a lamp unto my feet, and a light unto my path!

SEALING THE DEAL DECLARATION OF THE DAY!!

10. I John 3:22- I decree that whatsoever I ask of God I will receive, because I keep His commandments and do those things that are pleasing in His sight!

Day Thirty Four

1. Psalm 118:24 – This is the day which the Lord hath made, I will rejoice and be glad in it!

2. Isaiah 54:17 – I decree that my righteousness is of the Lord and no weapon formed against me today shall prosper!

3. Deuteronomy 1:30 – I decree that the Lord my God is going before me today and He will fight for me!

4. Psalm 68:1 – Today, God will arise in my life and every enemy will be scattered!

5. Proverbs 3:5 – Today, I will trust in the Lord with all my heart and lean not unto my own understanding!

6. Genesis 18:14 – I decree that there is nothing going on in my life right now that is too hard for the Lord to handle!

7. Nehemiah 4:6 – Today, I will not procrastinate or be slothful in taking care of my business, and my heart and my mind are positioned and prepared to do the work!

8. John 15:16 – I decree that God has chosen and ordained me and I will produce much fruit in this season and my fruit will remain and whatever I ask of the Father in Jesus name He will give it unto me!

9. Psalm 27:13 – Today, I will not faint, believing that the goodness of the Lord will manifest in my life while I am still living!

SEALING THE DEAL DECLARATION OF THE DAY!!

10. II Chronicles 6:40 – I decree that my declarations and prayers have gotten the attention of God and His eyes are open unto me and His ears are attentive to my cry today!

Day Thirty Five

1. Psalm 118:24 – This is the day which the Lord hath made, I will rejoice and be glad in it!

2. Isaiah 60:1 – Today, I will rise above every difficult situation in my life because the glory of the Lord is upon me and His light is shining in my life!

3. Luke 8:21 – Today, I will be sensitive to the voice of God, not only hearing but doing what He commands!

4. Psalm 8:6 – I decree that I have dominion power over the works of God's hands and all things are under my feet!

5. Acts 17:28 – I decree that I live, move and have my being in Jesus Christ!

6. Proverbs 16:7 – Today, I will ensure that my ways are pleasing unto the Lord and He will make my enemies to be at peace with me!

7. John 10:10 – Today, I embrace the abundant life that Jesus desires for me and I am living in the overflow!

8. Isaiah 43:19 – I will not miss the new thing that God is doing in my life in this season and I decree that it is springing forth right now. My direction is clear and every dry place is saturated with His presence!

9. James 4:8 – Today, I will draw near to God with clean hands and a pure heart and He will draw near to me!

SEALING THE DEAL DECLARATION OF THE DAY!!

10. Hebrews 10:23 – I will hold onto and be hopeful in the profession of my faith without wavering, knowing that God is faithful in all that He has promised me!

Day Thirty Six

1. Psalm 118:24 – This is the day which the Lord hath made, I will rejoice and be glad in it!

2. Isaiah 43:7 – I decree that I was formed by God and created for His glory!

3. Matthew 7:3 – Today, I will consider the beam that is in my eye before trying to pull out the mote that is in my brother's eye!

4. Ezekiel 37:14 – I decree that I will live today because the Spirit of God is in me and everything that He has spoken will be performed in my life!

5. Psalm 4:1 – Should I find myself in distress today I will call on God and pray, believing that He will have mercy on me and hear my prayer!

6. Proverbs 16:3 – Today, as I commit my works unto the Lord my thoughts shall be established!

7. Ephesians 1:17 – I decree that the Spirit of revelation and wisdom in the knowledge of God is being released to me today!

8. Deuteronomy 28:12 – I decree that the Lord is opening up heaven and releasing His good treasure unto me in this season. He is blessing the works of my hands and I am the lender and not the borrower!

9. Numbers 6:24-25 – I decree that today the Lord will bless me and keep me and make His face to shine upon me and He will be gracious unto me!

SEALING THE DEAL DECLARATION OF THE DAY!!

10. Jeremiah 1:12 – Because God is watching over His word to perform it, I am assured that the declarations which I have made today will manifest in my life and produce good results!

Day Thirty Seven

1. Psalm 118:24 – This is the day which the Lord hath made, I will rejoice and be glad in it!

2. Genesis 1:26 – Today, I embrace my dominion authority and will exercise it boldly knowing that I was created in the image and after the likeness of God!

3. Ephesians 3:20 – Today, the explosive power of God is working inside of me and I believe that my Father will do exceeding and abundantly above all that I ask or think!

4. Philippians 4:7 – I decree that I possess the peace of God which passeth all understanding and it shall keep my heart and mind through Christ Jesus!

5. James 5:16 – I decree that my prayers are effectual and fervent and they are producing great results in my life!

6. Matthew 11:28 – Today, I will find rest in God when I am faced with trials and challenges that are too heavy for me to bear!

7. Proverbs 18:21 – Today, I will choose my words carefully because there is power in my tongue to produce both life and death!

8. I Samuel 30:8 – In this new season I will pursue to recover everything that the enemy has stolen from me and I decree THAT WITHOUT FAIL I will recover ALL!

9. Matthew 5:16 – Today, I will let my light shine before men that they may see my good works and glorify my Father which is in heaven!

SEALING THE DEAL DECLARATION OF THE DAY!!

10. Ephesians 1:11 – I decree that God is working all things after the counsel of His own will; therefore as I have confessed His will through His word, I am confident that He will work it out and I will obtain my inheritance!

Day Thirty Eight

1. Psalm 118:24 – This is the day which the Lord hath made, I will rejoice and be glad in it!

2. II Timothy 1:7 – I decree the spirit of power, love and a sound mind over my life today and I refuse to allow fear to overtake or stop me because God has not given me THAT spirit!

3. Psalms 118:5 – Today, I will call upon the name of the Lord when I am in distress, knowing that He will set me in a large place!

4. Romans 8:6 – I decree that I am spiritually minded and life and peace are my portion!

5. Colossians 3:12-13 – Today, I will clothe myself with kindness, humbleness, meekness, longsuffering and forgiveness!

6. Titus 1:16 – I decree that I know God and I will not deny Him in my works!

7. Hebrews 10:35 – Today, I will not cast away my confidence, knowing that it will produce great rewards in my life!

8. Isaiah 54:2-3 – I decree that in this new season God is stretching and enlarging the place of my territory and I am breaking forth on the right hand and the left and will no longer dwell in small places!

9. Matthew 12:35 – Today, I will bring forth good things out of the good treasure of my heart!

SEALING THE DEAL DECLARATION OF THE DAY!!

10. Psalm 119:89-90 – I decree that the word of the Lord is settled in heaven and these declarations will stand firm in my life and establish that which I have spoken FOREVER!!

Day Thirty Nine

1. Psalm 118:24 – This is the day which the Lord hath made, I will rejoice and be glad in it!

2. Luke 10:19 – I decree that the enemy is under my feet and I am victorious over all of his power, and nothing by any means shall hurt me!

3. Philippians 2:13 – Today, God is working in me and creating a desire to will and do of His good pleasure!

4. Hebrews 11:6 – Today, I will exercise my faith because without it I cannot please God!

5. James 4:10 – Today, I will humble myself in the sight of the Lord and He will lift me up!

6. Proverbs 3:4 – I decree that I shall find favor and good understanding in the sight of God and man!

7. II Chronicles 20:12 – No matter what I come up against today I will not take my eyes off of God because He is with me!

8. Psalm 1:3 – I decree that this is my new season and I will bring forth fruit and whatever I do will prosper because I am positioned properly and walking in God's will!

9. Jeremiah- 1:19 – I decree victory over every area of my life and even though the enemy may fight against me he will not prevail!

SEALING THE DEAL DECLARATION OF THE DAY!!

10. Isaiah 55:11 – All of these declarations are God's word! Therefore, they shall not return unto me void, but will accomplish that which God pleases and purposes in my life!

Day Forty

1. Psalm 118:24 – This is the day which the Lord hath made, I will rejoice and be glad in it!

2. Romans 8:28 – Today, all things are working together for my good because I love God and I am called according to His purpose!

3. II Peter 1:3 – I decree that I have everything I need in order to be successful today because God has given me all things that pertain to life and godliness!

4. I John 5:4 – I decree by faith I am an overcomer because I am born of God and I believe in God!

5. II Timothy 2:1 – I decree that I am strong in the grace that is in Jesus Christ and nothing will stop me today!

6. Colossians 3:2 – Today, I will not be distracted by what I see as I set my affections on the things above and not on things of this world!

7. Job 33:12 – I decree that God is greater than man and He has the final say in my life!

8. Nehemiah 2:18 – In this new season the hand of God is upon me so I will RISE and BUILD and do the necessary work because God has strengthened my hands for this season!

9. Galatians 5:1 – Today, I will stand fast in the liberty in which Christ has made me free and I will not be entangled again in the bondage from my past!

SEALING THE DEAL DECLARATION OF THE DAY!!

10. Job 22:28 – I believe that all that I have decreed will be established unto me and the light of God shall be released in my life and be upon my ways according to His word!

CONCLUSION

Genesis 7:12- And the rain was upon the earth forty days and forty nights.

In the book of Genesis, we find the account of Noah and the ark. We all remember this story and recall how God executed judgment upon the earth by releasing torrential rain that flooded the earth. It was a heavy downpour that lasted for 40 days and 40 nights. Again, we see the number 40 representing a time of great turmoil and testing. This time of testing, just like all the others we previously discussed, did not last forever. It eventually came to an end. But the extraordinary thing about this particular time of testing is that God gave the people a tangible sign that He would never release this type of judgment upon the earth again.

Genesis 9:11- And I will establish my covenant with you, neither shall all flesh be cut off any more by the waters of a flood, neither shall there anymore be a flood to destroy the earth.

Genesis 9:16- And the bow shall be in the cloud, and I will look upon it that I may remember the everlasting covenant between God and every living creature of all flesh that is upon the earth.

God literally established an agreement with man that He would never flood the earth again. A covenant is just that, it is an agreement or a pledge that a certain promise or oath will be carried out. God thought enough about all creation to establish an everlasting covenant by way of the rainbow. Every time I see a rainbow, I am reminded of the faithfulness of God. He is a keeper of His word.

You have just completed 40 days of decreeing and declaring the word of God over your life. These past 40 days have most likely not been the easiest days of your life. I am sure that life's challenges showed up in the midst of your making a commitment to speak the words of eternal and divine life that are associated with these declarations. Inevitably so, the enemy is never pleased when God's people make up their minds to exercise their God-given privilege to stand upon the eternal promises found in God's word. When Jesus was in the wilderness for those forty days, guess who showed up? You got it...the devil! If he possessed the unmitigated gall to challenge Jesus, I am almost positive that he did not think twice about challenging you.

The wonderful thing is that you made it through. Just like Noah, I am sure there were some rocky days as you weathered the storms of life. I am sure you probably asked God along the way, "When is this storm going to end?" I am positive that you longed to see a glimpse of light shining at the end of a tunnel that seemed to hold an eternal darkness. But glory to God, you made it!

Noah took an uncommon risk and followed the direction of God in building the ark. He had never built an ark or experienced a flood, but he had faith enough in God to take Him at His word. I can hear Noah saying...*If God said it, I believe it, and that's the end of it.* I believe that you took an uncommon risk as you immersed yourself in the word of God over the past 40 days. I also believe that God has established a covenantal promise with you, just like He did during the days of Noah.

Hebrews 6:17-18 (Amplified):

17 - Accordingly God also, in His desire to show more convincingly and beyond doubt to those who were to inherit the promise the unchangeableness of His purpose and plan, intervened (mediated) with an oath.

18 - This was so that, by two unchangeable things (His promise and His oath) in which it is impossible for God ever to prove false or deceive us, we who have fled (to Him) for refuge might have mighty indwelling strength and strong encouragement to grasp and hold fast the hope appointed for us and set before us.

We have security in the fact that God is not a liar. It is not His intent to deceive or lead us astray. He gave us His word that we might have hope and be steadfast in our pursuit of what lies ahead for each of us. God does not change His mind or go back on the promises He has made to us through His word. He desires us to win in every situation. Not only does He desire us to win, He equips us to win. We have to believe that God is for us; knowing that He will accomplish His word in our lives.

I believe that you are going to begin to see tangible results based upon the words you have released into your life over the past 40 days! The words of these declarations are endowed with power from heaven. You must be convinced that the words you have spoken will begin to manifest heaven's agenda right here on earth. You must believe that what you have done at God's command will yield great results in your life. You have released the word of God over your family, faith, finances, and your future. Now, get ready to experience the fruit of your labor. God's word will not return empty. The word of God is bringing increase to your account in every capacity right now!

Isaiah 55:11- So shall the word be which goes forth out of my mouth; it shall not return unto me void, but it shall accomplish that which I please, and it shall prosper in the thing whereto I sent it.

You may have come to the END of this 40-day cycle of decreeing and declaring the word of God, but it is just the BEGINNING of a new season of your life in which you are going to begin to experience the miraculous power of God. God's word will not return void, it's going to bring good things into your life. With that being said, you should have an expectation for tangible, touchable, traceable evidences of the reality of the word of God you have confessed over the past 40 days.

It is important that you do not stop here. Continue to decree and declare the truths of God's word every day. You can even begin a new cycle of *40 Days of Decreeing and Declaring The Word of God*!! The word of God will always work, we just have to work it! You have confessed, believed, decreed, and declared! Now watch the word of God prosper on the inside of you and all around you!

ABOUT THE AUTHOR

Pastor Kimberly Jones is a "people lover" at heart, and it shows up in every aspect of her life. She is a co-pastor at Prevailing Love Worship Center in Stone Mountain, GA and owner of Living On Purpose Life & Relationship Coaching, LLC. In addition to being a Certified Professional Life Coach, Kimberly is also a motivational speaker, and spiritual mentor/mother to many. She uses her gifts and talents to encourage women and men to maximize their potential by taking ownership of their lives through spiritual awareness and personal development. Her speaking platforms include women's conferences, coaching seminars, and business workshops. She also works with individuals and groups as a Life Coach, compelling them to "Live on Purpose and Make Every Day Count."

Contact Kimberly online at www.kimberlyj.net or via email at livenow@kimberlyj.net.

Made in the USA
Lexington, KY
30 August 2019